Mud Pies

and

Dirt Cakes

A collection
of
chocolate delights.

Compiled by
Jackie Gannaway

Published in Austin, TX by COOKBOOK CUPBOARD, P.O. Box 50053, Austin, TX 78763 (512) 477-7070

ISBN 0-9629408-9-5

NOTICE: The information contained in this book is true, complete, and accurate to the best of my knowledge. All recommendations and suggestions are made without any guaranty on the part of the editor or Cookbook Cupboard. The editor and publisher disclaim any liability incurred in connection with the use of this information.

Artwork by Mosey 'N Me   1436 Baird Katy, Texas 77493   (713) 391-2281

Kitchen Crafts Collection

Jackie Gannaway

Mail Order Information

To order a copy of this book send a check for $3.95 + $1.50 for shipping (TX residents add 8 % sales tax) to Cookbook Cupboard, P.O. Box 50053, Austin, TX 78763. Send a note asking for this title by name. If you would like a descriptive list of all the fun titles in The Kitchen Crafts Collection, send a note asking for an order blank. One title chocolate lovers will be interested in is "Chocolate Crafts" - simple ways to make chocolate leaves, bowls, cups, chocolate dipped strawberries and much more. All the Kitchen Crafts titles are $3.95.

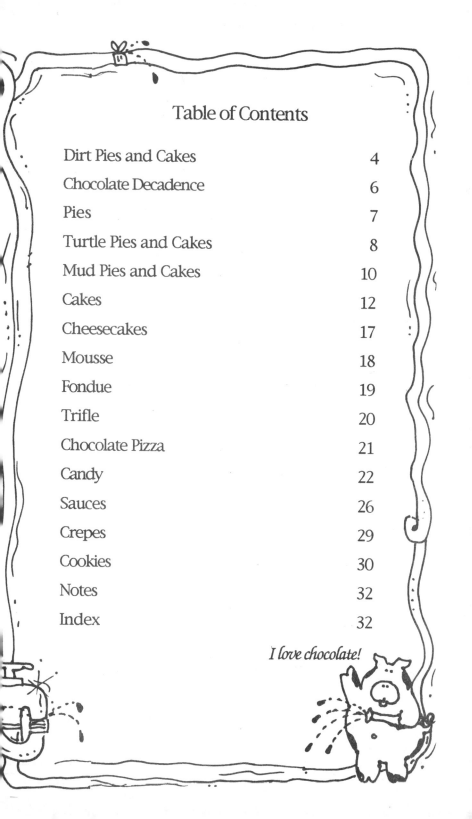

Table of Contents

Dirt Pies and Cakes   4

Chocolate Decadence   6

Pies   7

Turtle Pies and Cakes   8

Mud Pies and Cakes   10

Cakes   12

Cheesecakes   17

Mousse   18

Fondue   19

Trifle   20

Chocolate Pizza   21

Candy   22

Sauces   26

Crepes   29

Cookies   30

Notes   32

Index   32

I love chocolate!

Dirt Pie

1 cup milk
1 (4-serving size) chocolate
   instant pudding
1 (8oz) carton whipped
   topping, thawed
20 chocolate sandwich
   cookies, crushed

1 1/2 cups assorted "rocks"
   granola chunks, choc-
   olate chips, peanut
   butter chips, nuts
gummi worms. leaves,
   and flowers
1 graham cracker pie
   crust

1. Pour milk into medium bowl. Add pudding and beat
   with a whisk until well blended (1-2 minutes).
   Let stand 5 minutes.
2. Fold in whipped topping.
3. Stir in 1 cup of the cookies and all the "rocks".
4. Sprinkle with remaining cookie crumbs.
5. Freeze until firm (about 4 hours).
6. Garnish with gummi worms and decorations.
   Serves 6.

Dirt Cups

2 cups milk
1 (4 serving size) box chocolate instant pudding
1 (8 oz.) tub frozen whipped
   topping, thawed

1 (1 lb.) pkg. chocolate
   sandwich cookies,
   crushed
8 (9 oz.) plastic cups
gummi worms and frogs
peanuts or granola (opt.)

1. Mix milk and pudding in large bowl. Beat with a
   whisk until well blended. Let stand 5 minutes.
2. Add whipped topping and half the crushed cookies.
3. Place 1 Tb. crushed cookies in each cup. Fill cups
   3/4 full of pudding mixture. Top with remaining
   crushed cookies.
4. Chill at least 1 hour or until ready to serve. Decorate
   with "rocks" from peanuts or granola and
   "creatures" (gummi worms and frogs). Serves 8.

Flower Pot Dirt Cake

1 (1 lb. 4oz.) pkg. chocolate sandwich cookies
1 (8 oz.) block cream cheese
1/2 stick margarine
1 cup powdered sugar
3 cups milk
1 (6 serving) chocolate instant pudding
1 (12 oz.) carton frozen whipped topping, thawed
gummi worms, flowers, (silk or real), straws

1. Crush cookies in food processor until the crumbs resemble dirt. Set aside.
2. Mix cream cheese, margarine and powdered sugar in large bowl until well blended.
3. Mix milk and pudding in a large bowl, stirring until thickened.
4. Add whipped topping and blend. Add cream cheese mixture and mix well.
5. Line a large clean clay or plastic flower pot with foil.
6. Layer crumbs and pudding until flower pot is filled. End with crumbs. Chill.
7. Place silk flowers in straws and push into cake. Decorate with gummi worms. Serve with a scoop. Serves 8.

Individual Flower Pot Dirt Cakes

Use Dirt Cake recipe above, but instead of one large flower pot, use individual serving size flower pots. Line each one with foil and follow the directions for Dirt Cake.

Place flowers in straws and push into center of cake. Decorate with gummi worms or gummi flowers and leaves.

The recipe above fills 6 to 8 very small flower pots.

For Halloween, use vanilla pudding colored orange with food coloring and chocolate "dirt". Use lots of worms!

Sand Buckets

Use Dirt Cake recipe above, but instead of chocolate cookies and pudding, use vanilla. Use individual new plastic sand buckets or one large one. Line buckets with heavy duty foil. Serve with shovel that comes with the bucket.

Chocolate Decadence

16 (1 oz.) squares semi-sweet chocolate

1 1/2 sticks butter (no substitute)

5 eggs

1/4 cup sugar

2 Tb. flour

1. Melt chocolate with butter and sugar in top of a double boiler over simmering water.
2. Beat eggs with flour with electric mixer for 1 minute.
3. Gradually add melted chocolate mixture to egg mixture while beating with electric mixer. Continue to beat for 1 more minute.
4. Pour into a 9" springform pan lined with buttered wax paper.
5. Bake 20 minutes at 400. (It will not look done.)
6. Cool to room temperature. Remove sides from pan. Cover and refrigerate chocolate for 6 hours or overnight. Cut into very small wedges to serve. Clean knife under hot running water between each cut. Serve cold. Top with whipped cream or whipped cream and raspberry sauce (below).
Serves 10 to 12.

Raspberry Sauce

1 (10 oz.) box frozen raspberries, thawed

1/4 cup sugar

1/3 cup water

2 Tb. Cointreau or Grand Marnier

2 tsp. cornstarch

1. Pour raspberries into a strainer over a microsafe dish to catch juice.
2. Add sugar to juice. Stir and micro on High 2 minutes.
3. Measure 1/3 cup water in a small glass. Dissolve cornstarch in water. Add water mixture and liqueur to juice mixture and micro on High 2 minutes.
4. Add raspberries.
Refrigerate until ready to serve. Serve cold or micro 2 minutes to serve hot.

Toll House Pie

2 eggs
1/2 cup flour
1/2 cup sugar
1/2 cup packed brown
   sugar
1 cup butter, melted and
   cooled

1 (6 oz.) pkg. semisweet
   chocolate chips
1 cup chopped nuts
1 9" unbaked pie crust
whipped cream or
   ice cream to serve

1. Beat eggs with electric mixer.
2. Add flour and sugars. Mix well.
3. Blend in butter (at room temperature), chocolate
   chips and nuts.
4. Pour into pie crust and bake at 325 for 1 hour.
   Serve warm.
   Serves 6.

Fabulous Fudge Pie

1 cup butter
4 (1oz) squares unsweet-
   ened baking chocolate
2 cups sugar
1/2 cup sifted flour

4 eggs, beaten
1 tsp. vanilla
3/4 cup chopped pecans
ice cream or hot fudge
   sauce to serve (opt.)

1. Melt butter and chocolate in heavy pan over very low
   heat.
2. Combine sugar and flour in large bowl.
3. Add chocolate mixture to sugar mixture.
4. Beat in eggs and vanilla.
5. Stir in pecans.
6. Bake in a greased 10" pie pan for 25 minutes at 350.
7. Serve warm or at room temperature with ice cream
   or hot fudge sauce.
   Serves 6.

7

Chocolate Pecan Pie

1 (4oz) bar bittersweet chocolate, broken into pieces
1/4 cup butter
2/3 cup light corn syrup
3 eggs
1 Tb. vanilla or bourbon
1/4 tsp. salt
1/2 cup packed brown sugar
1 cup pecan halves
9" unbaked pie crust
whipped topping (opt.)

1. Melt chocolate, butter and corn syrup in heavy pan over very low heat, stirring constantly.
2. Beat eggs with vanilla and salt.
3. Stir in sugar, chocolate mixture and nuts.
4. Pour into pie shell. Bake 1 at 400 for 10 minutes. Reduce heat to 350 and continue baking 30-35 more minutes. Cool. Serve with whipped topping, if desired. Can add 1 Tb. bourbon to the filling. Serves 6.

Turtle Pie

1 cup caramel candies (20)
1/2 cup whipping cream, divided
2 cups pecan pieces
3/4 cup semisweet chocolate chips
1/4 cup whipping cream
1 chocolate crumb crust

1. Melt caramels in a heavy pan over low heat, stirring frequently.
2. Add 1/2 cup whipping cream and mix well.
3. Remove from heat and add pecans.
4. Spread in crust and refrigerate until set.
5. Melt chocolate chips over simmering water in double boiler. Mix in 1/4 cup cream.
6. Drizzle chocolate mixture over pie. Refrigerate at least 1 hour. Serves 6.

Turtle Cake Squares

1 (14oz) pkg. caramels
1 (5oz) can evaporated
  milk
1/2 cup butter, melted

1 German chocolate cake
  mix
1 cup finely chopped nuts
1 (12 oz.) pkg. chocolate
  chips

1. Melt caramels and 1/4 cup milk in heavy pan over
   low heat, stirring constantly. Set aside.
2. Combine melted butter, dry cake mix, nuts and
   remaining milk in large bowl.
3. Press half of this mixture into a greased 9" x 13" pan.
4. Bake 6 minutes at 325.
5. Remove from oven - sprinkle chocolate chips on top.
6. Spread caramel mixture over chocolate chips.
7. Press remaining cake mixture over caramel.
8. Bake 15-18 more minutes.
9. Cool and cut into squares. Serves 12.

Turtle Cake

1 German chocolate cake
  mix
3 eggs
1 1/4 cups water
1/3 cup oil
1 (14 oz.) bag caramels

1 (5 oz.) can evaporated
  milk
1/2 cup butter
1 (12 oz.) bag semisweet
  chocolate chips
1 1/2 cups chopped nuts

1. Make cake mix with eggs, water and oil according to
   pkg. directions. Pour 1/2 the batter into a greased
   and floured 9" x 13" pan. Bake at 350 for 20 minutes.
2. Place caramels, evaporated milk and butter in large
   pan. Stir over low heat until blended and creamy.
3. Pour caramel mixture over top of warm cake.
4. Sprinkle chocolate chips and 1 cup of chopped nuts
   over caramel mixture.
5. Pour remaining batter on top and sprinkle with
   remaining nuts. Bake at 350 for 20 more minutes.
   Serves 12.

Mississippi Mud Pie

1 (4oz) bar sweet baking
   chocolate
1 stick butter
3 eggs
3 Tb. light corn syrup
1 cup sugar
1 tsp. vanilla
1/8 tsp. salt
9" unbaked deep dish
   pie crust
1 pint vanilla ice cream

1. Melt chocolate and butter in heavy pan over low
   heat.
2. Beat eggs - add corn syrup, sugar and vanilla.
3. Add egg mixture to chocolate mixture. Pour into
   pie crust.
4. Bake 35-40 minutes at 350. Top will be cracked and
   the filling will be soft. Cool to room temperature.
5. Serve with ice cream.
   Serves 6.

Mississippi Mud Brownies

1 fudge brownie mix
2 eggs
1/3 cup water
1/3 cup oil
1 (7 oz) jar marshmallow
   creme
1 (16 oz.) container milk
   chocolate frosting

1. Combine brownie mix, eggs, water and oil in large
   bowl. Stir until well blended.
2. Bake in a sprayed 9" x 13" pan at 350 for 25-28
   minutes.
3. Spread marshmallow creme gently over hot
   brownies.
4. Melt frosting in double boiler. Pour 1 1/4 cups melted
   frosting over marshmallow creme. Swirl with a
   knife to marble.
5. Cool completely. Cut into squares.
   Serves 8.

Mississippi Mud Cake

2 sticks butter
2 cups sugar
4 eggs
1 1/2 cups flour
1/2 tsp. salt
1/3 cup cocoa powder

1/2 cup chopped pecans
1 cup flaked coconut
1 tsp. vanilla
3 cups miniature marsh-
mallows

1. Cream butter and sugar with an electric mixer in a large bowl.
2. Add eggs, one at a time, beating well each time.
3. Place flour, salt and cocoa into a medium bowl. Blend with a whisk.
4. Add dry ingredients to butter mixture. Mix with electric mixer on low until blended.
5. Mix in pecans, coconut and vanilla.
6. Bake in a greased and floured 9" x 13" pan at 350 for 30 to 35 minutes.
7. Sprinkle top with marshmallows. Return to oven just until marshmallows are melted and lightly browned. Serves 12.

Frosting

1 stick butter
1 (16 oz.) box powdered
sugar

1/3 cup cocoa powder
1/3 cup evaporated milk

1. Melt butter in large pan.
2. Place powdered sugar and cocoa in a large bowl and blend with a whisk.
3. Stir half the sugar mixture into the melted butter along with the milk. Mix well.
4. Pour hot mixture over remaining sugar and beat well.
5. Spread frosting over top of warm cake. Let stand until cool. Cover and refrigerate 8 hours or overnight. Serves 12.

11

Buttermilk Fudge Cake

2 1/2 cups flour
2 cups sugar
1/2 tsp. salt
1 tsp. cinnamon (opt.)
1 cup shortening
3 eggs

1 tsp. vanilla
1/3 cup cocoa
2 tsp. soda
1 cup buttermilk
1 cup boiling water

1. Mix flour, sugar, salt and cinnamon in medium bowl.
2. Place shortening, eggs, vanilla and cocoa in large bowl. Cream with electric mixer.
3. Mix soda with buttermilk.
4. Add dry ingredients to creamed mixture, alternately with buttermilk.
5. Add boiling water and mix well.
6. Bake in sprayed 9" x 13" pan at 350 for 1 hour. Serves 12.

Frosting

1 stick margarine
3 Tb. cocoa
6 Tb. milk

1 (16 oz.) box powdered sugar
1 tsp. vanilla
1 cup chopped nuts (opt.)

1. Melt margarine with cocoa and milk over low heat.
2. Pour this mixture over powdered sugar in large bowl.
3. Add vanilla and nuts and mix well.
4. Pour over hot cake.

Texas Sheet Cake

1 cup butter
1/4 cup cocoa
1 cup water
2 cups flour
1 1/2 cups brown sugar
1 tsp. baking soda

1 tsp. cinnamon
1/2 tsp. salt
1 (14 oz.) can sweetened
  condensed milk, divided
2 eggs
1 tsp. vanilla

1. Melt butter, cocoa and water in small pan over low heat. Bring to a boil and then set aside.
2. Mix flour, brown sugar, soda, cinnamon and salt in large bowl.
3. Add butter mixture to dry ingredients and mix well.
4. Add 1/3 cup sweetened condensed milk, eggs and vanilla. Mix well.
5. Bake in greased and floured 9" x 13" pan for 20 minutes at 350.
   Serves 12.

Frosting

1/2 stick butter
1/4 cup cocoa
remaining sweetened con-
  densed milk from above

1 cup powdered sugar
1 cup chopped nuts

1. Melt butter with cocoa and milk in medium pan. Remove from heat.
2. Add powdered sugar and mix until smooth.
3. Spread on cooled cake. Sprinkle with nuts.

13

Tunnel of Fudge Cake

3 1/2 sticks butter, softened
1 3/4 cup sugar
6 eggs
2 cups powdered sugar

2 1/4 cups flour
3/4 cup cocoa
2 cups chopped nuts,
  (must include)

1. Cream butter and sugar in large bowl with electric mixer until light and fluffy.
2. Add eggs one at a time, beating well after each.
3. Add powdered sugar, a little at a time, mixing well.
4. Add flour, cocoa, and nuts and mix by hand.
5. Bake in greased and floured Bundt or tube pan at 350 for 1 hour.
6. Cool in pan 1 hour. Remove from pan and cool completely.
   Serves 12.

Optional Glaze

3/4 cup powdered sugar
1/4 cup cocoa

2 to 3 Tb. milk

1. Mix all ingredients in a small bowl until well blended.
2. Drizzle over cooled cake.

Miracle Whip® Chocolate Cake

1 chocolate cake mix
1/2 cup cocoa
3 eggs

1 1/3 cups water
1 cup Miracle Whip®
  salad dressing

1. Mix cake mix and cocoa.
2. Add remaining ingredients and mix with electric mixer until well blended.
3. Bake in greased and floured 9" x 13" pan at 350 for 30-40 minutes
4. Can frost with one of the frostings on pages 12 or 13.
   Serves 12.

14

Chocolate Sour Cream Pound Cake

2 sticks butter, softened
2 cups sugar
1 cup packed brown
   sugar
6 eggs

2 tsp. vanilla
2 1/2 cups flour
1/4 tsp. baking soda
1/2 cup cocoa
1 cup sour cream

1. Cream butter and sugars in large bowl with electric mixer for 5 minutes.
2. Add eggs, one at a time, beating until just mixed.
3. Add vanilla.
4. Mix flour, soda and cocoa in medium bowl. Blend with a whisk.
5. Add flour mixture to butter mixture alternately with sour cream, beginning and ending with flour. Mix at low speed after each addition.
6. Bake in greased and floured tube pan at 325 for 1 hour and 20 minutes .
7. Cool in pan 10 minutes. Remove from pan and cool completely. Serves 12.

Fudge Pudding Cake

1 cup Bisquick®
1/4 cup cocoa
1 (14oz) can sweetened
   condensed milk, divided
3/4 cup chocolate syrup, divided

1 tsp. vanilla
1/2 cup hot water
whipped topping or
   ice cream to serve

1. Combine Bisquick and cocoa in large bowl. Mix in 1 cup sweetened condensed milk, 1/4 cup chocolate syrup and vanilla. Mix until blended.
2. Spoon into greased 8" square pan.
3. Combine remaining sweetened condensed milk, chocolate syrup and hot water in small bowl.
4. Pour liquid mixture over mixture in pan. Do not stir.
5. Bake at 375 for 25-30 minutes. Let stand 15 minutes.
6. Spoon into dessert dishes with pudding over the top. Serves 8.

Milky Way® Cake

8 Milky Way® candy bars
   (2.15 oz each)
1 cup butter or margarine
2 cups sugar
4 eggs, separated
1 1/4 cups buttermilk

1/2 tsp. baking soda
2 1/2 cups flour
1/2 tsp. salt
1 cup chopped pecans
6 (1 oz.) squares
   semisweet chocolate

1. Place candy bars and butter in a large heavy pan. Melt over very low heat, stirring often. Remove from heat and add sugar.
2. Place egg yolks, buttermilk and baking soda in a small bowl. Mix until blended.
3. Mix flour and salt in another bowl.
4. Add flour mixture to candy mixture alternately with buttermilk mixture. Begin and end with dry ingredients. Stir in pecans.
5. Beat egg whites in large bowl with electric mixer until stiff, but not dry. Blend into batter. Pour into a greased and floured tube pan. Bake at 325 for 1 1/4 hours. Cool on rack 15 minutes. Remove from pan and cool completely.
6. Melt chocolate over simmering water in double boiler. Spread over cooled cake.
Serves 12.

German Chocolate Cheesecake

Filling:
3 (8 oz.) blocks cream
    cheese, softened
3/4 cup sugar
1/4 cup cocoa
2 tsp. vanilla
3 eggs, beaten
1 extra large graham crust

Topping:
2 Tb. butter
1/4 cup evaporated milk
2 Tb. brown sugar
1 egg yolk, beaten
1/2 tsp. vanilla
1/2 cup chopped pecans
1/2 cup coconut

1. Mix cream cheese, sugar, cocoa and vanilla in large
   bowl with electric mixer until light and fluffy.
2. Add eggs, one at a time mixing well.
3. Pour into crust. Bake at 350 for 35 minutes.
4. Cool completely before adding topping.
5. To make topping - melt butter in medium pan over
   low heat. Add milk, sugar, egg yolk and vanilla.
6. Cook, stirring constantly, until thickened.
7. Add pecans and coconut. Spread on cooled
   cheesecake. Chill 2 hours or overnight. Serves 8.

Chocolate Cheesecake

2 (8oz) blocks cream
    cheese, softened
1/2 cup sugar
3 eggs

1 1/2 cups semisweet
    chocolate chips
1 chocolate or graham
    cracker pie crust
1/2 cup sour cream

1. Mix cream cheese and sugar in large bowl with
   electric mixer until light and fluffy.
2. Add eggs, one at a time, beating well each time.
3. Melt 3/4 cup chocolate chips over simmering water
   in double boiler. Add to cream cheese mixture,
   beating until thick and smooth.
4. Spread in pie crust and bake 30-35 minutes at 350.
5. Melt remaining 3/4 cup chocolate chips. Mix with
   sour cream. Spread over cooled pie.
6. Chill 4 hours or overnight. Serves 6.

17

Chocolate Mousse

4 (1oz) squares unsweet-
   ened chocolate
4 egg whites
1 cup whipping cream

3/4 cup powdered
   sugar
1/2 tsp. vanilla or rum
whipped cream (opt.)
chocolate shavings (opt.)

1. Melt chocolate over simmering water in double
   boiler. Let cool to 110, set aside.
2. Beat egg whites until stiff - set aside.
3. Beat whipping cream until frothy. Gradually add
   powdered sugar, beating until stiff peaks form. Mix
   in vanilla and fold cream mixture into egg whites.
4. Add cooled chocolate and mix gently until blended.
5. Spoon into individual serving dishes or glasses.
6. Refrigerate at least 2 hours.
7. Serve with whipped cream and chocolate shavings.
   Serves 4.

Pots de Creme

2 cups half and half cream
2 eggs, lightly beaten
2 Tb. sugar
3 cups semisweet
   chocolate chips

3 Tb. amaretto
   or 2 Tb. rum
2 tsp. vanilla
1/8 tsp. salt
whipped topping (opt.)

1. Combine first 3 ingredients in a heavy pan. Cook over
   medium heat 12 minutes or until temperature
   reaches 160.
2. Add chocolate chips and next 3 ingredients, stirring
   until smooth.
3. Spoon into 5 or 6 individual serving dishes. Cover and
   chill. Top with whipped topping if desired.

Chocolate Fondue

3 (3 - 3/5 oz) bars Swiss
   milk chocolate

1/2 cup whipping cream
2 Tb. Cointreau or brandy

1. Place first three ingredients in a double boiler.
   Heat and stir until well blended.
2. Place in fondue pot.
   Serves 6.

Dippers for both fondues:

Apple slices, pear slices, bananas, (generously sprinkle apples, pears and bananas with lemon juice to keep from turning brown), strawberries, marshmallows, pound cake cubes, shortbread cookies, vanilla wafers.

After dipping fruit in chocolate, dip in individual dishes of coconut, cocoa powder, sugar, slivered almonds, cinnamon, if desired.

Caramel Chocolate Fondue

1 (14oz) can sweetened
   condensed milk
1 (12-16 oz) jar caramel
   topping

1 (6 oz.) pkg. semisweet
   chocolate chips
1/4 cup brandy

1. Mix first 3 ingredients in heavy pan. Cook, stirring, over low heat until chocolate melts.
2. Blend in brandy.
3. Place in a fondue pot.
   Serves 10.

Chocolate Trifle

1 fudge brownie mix
eggs
oil
water
1/2 cup coffee flavored
    liqueur
2 (6 serving size) boxes
    chocolate instant pudding

6 cups milk
1 (12 oz.) tub frozen
    whipped topping,
    thawed
6 (1.4 oz.) English toffee
    flavored candy bars,
    crushed

1. Prepare and bake brownie mix with eggs, oil and
    water according to package directions.
2. Prick top of warm brownies thoroughly with a fork.
3. Drizzle brownies with liqueur. Cool brownies and
    crumble.
4. Prepare pudding with milk according to package
    directions. Don't chill the pudding.
5. Place 1/3 of the crumbled brownies in bottom of 3
    quart clear glass dish or serving bowl. Top with 1/3
    of the pudding, whipped topped and crushed candy
    bars. Repeat layers twice, ending with crushed
    candy bars.
6. Chill 8 hours or overnight.
    Serves 16 to 18.

Chocolate Dessert Pizza

1 (20 oz.) roll refrigerated chocolate chip cookie dough
1 cup mini marshmallows
1/2 cup semisweet chocolate chips
1/2 cup chopped pecans

1. Grease a 12" pizza pan.
2. Slice cookie dough into 1/4" slices. Cover pizza pan with cookie dough slices. Press together and spread to form a continuous crust.
3. Bake at 350 for 8 minutes.
4. Remove from oven and sprinkle evenly with chocolate chips, pecans and marshmallows.
5. Return to oven for 5 more minutes. Place under the broiler to brown marshmallows. Cool completely. Cut into wedges.
Serves 8.

Chocolate Crispy Pizza

1 (12 oz.) pkg. semisweet chocolate chips
16 oz. white almond bark, divided
2 cups mini marshmallows
1 cup crisp rice cereal
1 cup chopped peanuts
1 (6 oz.) jar maraschino cherries
1/3 cup coconut
1 tsp. oil

1. Melt chocolate chips with 14 oz. almond bark over simmering water in double boiler, stirring until smooth. Remove from heat.
2. Stir in marshmallows, cereal and peanuts.
3. Pour onto greased 12" pizza pan. Top with halved cherries and sprinkle with coconut.
4. Melt remaining almond bark with oil over low heat, stirring until smooth, Drizzle melted almond bark over coconut. Chill until firm. Store at room temperature.
Serves 8.

Rocky Road Candy

1 (12oz) pkg. semisweet
    chocolate ships
1 (14oz) can sweetened
    condensed milk
2 Tb. butter

2 cups pecans, walnuts
    or peanuts
1 (10 oz.) pkg. miniature
    marshmallows

1. Melt chocolate, milk and butter over simmering
    water in a double boiler. Cook, stirring constantly,
    until creamy.
2. Remove from heat and add nuts and marshmallows.
3. Pour onto a wax paper lined 9" x 13" pan.
4. Cut into squares. Store in refrigerator. You can toast
    the nuts first, if desired.

English Toffee

1 cup sugar
2 sticks butter
    (no substitute)

1 to 2 cups almond or
    pecan pieces
1 (6 oz.) pkg. semisweet
    chocolate chips

1. Cook sugar, butter and nuts over medium heat,
    stirring constantly, for 14 minutes or until brown.
2. Pour mixture onto baking sheet.
3. Sprinkle chocolate chips on top of hot mixture
    and spread chocolate as it melts.
4. Refrigerate. Break or cut into squares.

Chocolate Bourbon Balls

1 (6oz) pkg. semisweet
  chocolate chips
1/2 cup bourbon
3 Tb. light corn syrup
2 1/2 cups vanilla wafer
  crumbs

1/2 cup sifted powdered
  sugar
1 cup finely chopped nuts
sugar

1. Melt chocolate chips over simmering water in double
   boiler. Remove from heat.
2. Stir in bourbon and corn syrup - set aside.
3. In a large bowl, mix crumbs, powdered sugar and
   pecans.
4. Add chocolate mixture to crumb mixture - let stand 30
   minutes.
5. Shape into 1" balls. Roll in sugar.
6. Store in airtight container in refrigerator.
   Better flavor after a week.

Pecan Bourbon Candy

1 stick butter
2 cups powdered sugar
1/3 cup bourbon, rum
  or brandy

3 cups pecan halves
8 (1 oz.) squares semi-
  sweet chocolate

1. Cream half of the butter in a large bowl with electric
   mixer.
2. Add sugar and liquor alternately, beating until thick
   and smooth.
3. Shape mixture into acorn sized balls.
4. Press a pecan half on each side of the ball. Chill 20
   minutes.
5. Melt chocolate with 1 1/2 tsp. butter over simmering
   water in double boiler.
6. Dip one end of each candy in chocolate and place on
   cookie sheet. Chill until firm.

23

Chocolate Marshmallow Fudge

3/4 cup evaporated milk
1/2 cup butter, cut in pieces
2 cups sugar
1/4 tsp. salt
1 (12 oz.) pkg, semisweet
    chocolate chips

2 cups miniature
    marshmallows
1 tsp. vanilla
1 cup chopped nuts

1. In heavy pan heat milk and butter until melted.
2. Add sugar and salt, stirring constantly until it starts
    to boil. Cook on low heat, stirring, 2 minutes.
3. Remove from heat. Add chocolate chips and
    marshmallows, beating until smooth and thick.
4. Add vanilla and nuts. Spread into a buttered 9" square
    pan. Chill 2 hours or until firm. Cut into squares.

Chocolate Fudge

3 cups chocolate chips
1 (14 oz.) can sweetened
    condensed milk

dash salt
2 tsp. vanilla
1 cup chopped nuts

1. Place chocolate chips, milk and salt in a heavy pan.
    Melt over low heat. Stir until chocolate is
    completely melted.
2. Add vanilla and nuts.
3. Spread in greased 8" square pan. Refrigerate until
    firm. Cut into squares.

Chocolate Truffles

4 (1 oz.) squares semi-
    sweet chocolate
3 Tb. butter

1 1/2 Tb. amaretto or
    Grand Marnier
2 Tb. Ghiradelli Ground
    Chocolate®

1. Melt chocolate over simmering water in a double
    boiler, stirring constantly.
2. Remove from heat and add butter, stirring until
    melted.
3. Add liqueur. Chill until firm enough to shape into
    small oval pieces.
4. Roll in ground chocolate. Cover and chill overnight.
    Makes 18 truffles.

Mocha Almond Truffles

4 (1 oz.) squares unsweet-
    ened chocolate
1 tsp. butter
1/3 cup powdered sugar

1/3 cup almond paste
1 Tb. strong hot coffee
1/4 cup cocoa mixed with
1 tsp. cinnamon

1. Melt chocolate and butter over simmering water in
    double boiler.
2. Blend in sugar, almond paste and coffee until smooth.
3. Add a little more powdered sugar if needed for stiff-
    ness. Shape into half-inch balls and roll in cocoa
    and cinnamon mixture.
4. Place on waxed paper and chill.

Milky Way® Sauce

12 oz. Milky Way® candy
    bars, cut up
1 cup milk

6 (1 oz.) squares semi-
    sweet chocolate, broken
1 1/3 cups chopped nuts

1. Mix candy, milk and chocolate over boiling water in a double boiler.
2. Cook, stirring constantly, until melted and smooth.
3. Add nuts.
4. Serve warm over ice cream. Store in refrigerator and reheat over very low heat.

Caramel Fudge Sauce

1/3 cup milk
1 (16 oz.) pkg, caramels
3/4 cup semisweet chocolate
    chips

1 cup vanilla ice cream
1 tsp. vanilla

1. Melt caramels with milk over boiling water in double boiler, stirring until smooth.
2. Add chocolate chips and stir until melted.
3. Mix in ice cream and vanilla.

    Serve warm over ice cream.

Caramel Turtle Topping

vanilla ice cream
caramel ice cream topping

chopped pecans
chocolate Magic Shell®
    topping

1. Sprinkle chopped pecans on top of each serving of ice cream.
2. Heat both toppings very briefly in microwave to soften.
3. Spoon caramel topping and then chocolate topping over ice cream.

Cherry Fudge Sauce

1 (6 oz.) jar maraschino
   cherries

1/2 cup chocolate
   fudge sauce (not
   chocolate syrup)

1. Drain cherries and save syrup. Place cherries in food processor.
2. Add fudge sauce and 2 tsp. of the cherry syrup.
3. Process briefly until blended and cherries are finely chopped.

This sauce is excellent heated in the microwave.

This can be made with 1/2 cup mandarin orange segments instead of cherries.

Chocolate Sauce

3 (1 oz.) squares unsweetened chocolate
1 Tb. butter
1 cup sugar

1 (5 oz.) can evaporated
   milk
1/2 tsp. vanilla

1. Melt chocolate and butter in small heavy pan.
2. Add sugar and milk. Cook, stirring frequently until thick. Add vanilla. Serve warm.

Brownie Sundae

Place a brownie in an individual dessert dish. Top with sliced fresh strawberries and kiwis. Top with a scoop of vanilla ice cream and drizzle with heated chocolate fudge sauce.

Chocolate Cream Cheese

1 (8 oz.) block cream cheese,   1/2 cup Ghiradelli
     room temperature   Ground Chocolate®
1/2 tsp. vanilla

1. Mix all ingredients in a medium bowl with electric
    mixer until well blended.
2. Place in a small serving dish and chill.

Serve with crackers or fruit bread. Also good on fresh
fruit pieces.

Chocolate Butter

2 Tb. cocoa powder   1 stick butter, softened
1/4 cup powdered sugar   1/8 tsp. vanilla

1. Mix cocoa powder and powdered sugar in small bowl.
2. Cream butter with electric mixer in a medium bowl.
3. Sift sugar mixture into butter through a strainer.
4. Add vanilla.
5. Mix with mixer 1 minute until well blended.
6. Place in small crock. Refrigerate until needed.
    Let sit at room temperature 15 minutes before
    serving.

Serve on toast, English muffins, scones.

Chocolate Crepes

2 (1 oz.) squares semi-   2 Tb. sugar
  sweet chocolate   1 Tb. brandy
1 Tb. butter or margarine 1/4 tsp. salt
1 cup milk   1 cup flour
2 eggs

1. In heavy pan, melt chocolate with butter over very low heat, stirring constantly.
2. Place milk, eggs, sugar, brandy and salt in blender and mix. Blend in flour and mix.
3. Add chocolate mixture, blending until smooth.
4. Chill 2 hours .
5. Make 1 crepe at a time in a sprayed nonstick skillet or crepe pan over medium heat. Make each crepe with a heaping Tb. batter, tilting pan to spread batter thin. Spray skillet between each crepe and add water to batter if it becomes too thick.
6. Stack finished crepes on a plate and keep covered with a damp paper towel. Finished crepes can be wrapped well in plastic wrap and refrigerated for a few days. To reheat, wrap in foil and heat at 350 for 5 minutes.

Fill crepes with sweetened whipped cream or vanilla ice cream. Fold over and top with heated fudge ice cream topping.

Makes 16 small crepes.

Chocolate Cherry Cookies

1 (12oz) pkg. semisweet
   chocolate chips
1/2 cup butter
1 cup packed brown sugar
1 egg
1 tsp. vanilla

2 cups flour
1 tsp. baking powder
1/2 tsp. salt
1 (16 oz.) jar maraschino
   cherries
2 Tb. syrup from cherries
1 Tb. butter

1. Melt 1 cup chocolate chips over simmering water in double boiler.
2. Place butter and sugar in a large bowl. Cream with electric mixer.
3. Add egg, vanilla and melted chocolate, beating until smooth.
4. Combine flour with baking powder and salt. Add to creamed mixture, beating until smooth.
5. Chill 1 hour or longer. Enclose a cherry in 1 Tb. dough.
6. Bake on greased baking sheet for 12-14 minutes at 350.
7. Melt remaining chocolate chips with cherry syrup and 1 Tb. butter. Frost top of cookies.

Makes approximately 40 cookies.

Chocolate Butter Cookies

1/2 cup sugar
1 1/2 sticks butter,
  softened
1 egg yolk

1 tsp. almond extract
1 1/2 cups flour
1/4 cup cocoa powder

1. Combine sugar, butter, egg yolk and extract in large bowl. Mix with electric mixer on medium speed until light and fluffy.
2. Gradually add flour and cocoa and mix until well blended.
3. Shape by teaspoons into balls, logs or flattened balls.
4. Place 1" apart on baking sheets.
5. Bake at 375 for 7 to 9 minutes.
   Decorate as desired with melted chocolate, sprinkles, colored sugar. This dough can be used in a cookie press. Makes 3 dozen.

English Toffee Cookies

1 cup brown sugar
1 cup butter flavored
  shortening
1 egg yolk

1 1/2 cups flour
1/2 cup chopped nuts
6 (1.55 oz.) milk chocolate
  candy bars

1. Cream sugar and shortening with electric mixer.
2. Add egg yolk, flour and nuts. Mix well.
3. Spread dough very thinly on a large baking sheet with sides.
4. Bake at 350 for 20 minutes or until barely brown.
5. Take out of oven and immediately place unwrapped candy bars over the top. Spread melted chocolate while still warm. Cut cookies into squares while still warm.

Life is short - eat dessert first!

Chocolate Notes

A 6 oz. package of chocolate chips equals one cup.
A 12 oz. package of chocolate chips equals two cups.
Chocolate for baking and cooking comes in 1 ounce squares
and in bars marked off in 1/2 ounce sections.
Flavors are unsweetened, bittersweet, semisweet and sweet
(often called German's sweet).
Chocolate can be melted over direct heat and in the microwave.
The danger in melting chocolate is getting it too hot. It will
harden and can even burn if it gets too hot. The most foolproof
way is in a double boiler over simmering, not boiling water.

Index

Bourbon Balls	23
Brownie Sundae	27
Buttermilk Fudge Cake	12
Cakes	12-16
Candy	22-25
Caramel Choc. Fondue	19
Caramel Fudge Sauce	26
Caramel Turtle Topping	26
Cherry Fudge Sauce	27
Choc. Bourbon Balls	23
Choc. Sour Cream Cake	15
Chocolate Butter	28
Chocolate Butter Cookies	31
Chocolate Cheesecake	17
Chocolate Cherry Cookies	30
Chocolate Cream Cheese	28
Chocolate Crepes	29
Chocolate Decadence	6
Chocolate Fondue	19
Chocolate Fudge	24
Chocolate Mousse	18
Chocolate Pecan Pie	8
Chocolate Pizza	21
Chocolate Sauce	27
Chocolate Trifle	20
Chocolate Truffles	25
Cookies	30
Crepes	29
Decadence	6
Dessert Pizza	21
Dirt Cups	4
Dirt Pie	4
English Toffee	22
English Toffee Cookies	31
Fabulous Fudge Pie	7
Flower Pot Dirt Cake	5
Fudge	24
Fudge Pie	7
Fudge Pudding Cake	15
German Chocolate Cheesecake	17
Milky Way Cake	16
Milky Way Sauce	26
Miracle Whip Cake	14
Miss. Mud Brownies	10
Mississippi Mud Cake	14
Mississippi Mud Pie	10
Mocha Almond Truffles	25
Pecan Bourbon Candy	23
Pies	7-10
Pots de Creme	18
Pudding Cake	15
Raspberry Sauce	6
Rocky Road Candy	22
Sand Buckets	5
Sauces	26-28
Texas Sheet Cake	13
Toll House Pie	7
Trifle	20
Truffles	25
Tunnel of Fudge Cake	14
Turtle Cake	9
Turtle Cake Squares	9
Turtle Pie	9